BLOOD

TOMY WALMSLEY

Blood
first published 2000 by
Scirocco Drama
An imprint of J. Gordon Shillingford Publishing Inc.
© 1999 Tom Walmsley

Scirocco Drama Series Editor: Glenda MacFarlane
Cover design by Terry Gallagher/Doowah Design Inc.
Author photo by Pamela Stewart
Printed and bound in Canada

We acknowledge the financial support of The Canada Council for the Arts and the Manitoba Arts Council for our publishing program.

All rights reserved. No part of this book may be reproduced, for any reason, by any means, without the permission of the publisher. This play is fully protected under the copyright laws of Canada and all other countries of the Copyright Union and is subject to royalty. Changes to the text are expressly forbidden without written consent of the author. Rights to produce, film, record in whole or in part, in any medium or in any language, by any group amateur or professional, are retained by the author.
Production inquiries should be addressed to:
Charles Northcote, Literary Agent
The Core Group Talent Agency Inc.
3 Church Street, Suite 507, Toronto, ON M5E 1M2
phone (416) 955-0819 Fax (416) 955-0532
e-mail: charlie@coregroupta.com

Canadian Cataloguing in Publication Data

Walmsley, Tom, 1948-
    Blood

A Play.
ISBN 1-896239-64-1

    I. Title.

PS8595.A583B59 2000   C812'.54   C00-900170-0
PR9199.3.W348B59 2000

Blood

Acknowledgements

I wrote a memoir of my sister shortly after she died. It was written at the suggestion of Julia Sasso, who performed it as a dance piece. Laurie Hood wrote and performed the music and I read the text aloud. The piece was called *Maxine* and it was produced in Peterborough, Ottawa and Toronto.

I revised the text slightly and read it for broadcast on the CBC. William Lane was the producer and Nic Gotham accompanied the reading on saxophone.

That piece became the starting point for *Blood*. The play is not autobiographical, but my relationship to my sister is its root.

David Ferry moved heaven and earth to make it possible for me to write the play. I have a wretched way of expressing gratitude, but I will be forever grateful to David for his efforts.

The part of Noelle was written for Kyra Harper. She gave me the voice, she showed me the way, she was astounding. She gave me my sister.

I owe all of these people every scrap of gratitude I own in my dark little heart.

Tom Walmsley's plays include *Something Red* and *The Jones Boy*. He writes screenplays and is the author of *Shades*, a novel.

Production Credits

Blood premiered at Factory Theatre, Toronto, on November 22, 1995 with the following cast:

NOELLE TERRY .... Kyra Harper
CHRIS TERRY .... John Evans

Directed by David Ferry
Set design by Graeme S. Thomson and Leslie Commins
Light design by Graeme S. Thomson
Costume design by Minda Johnson
Sound design by David Ferry
Stage Manager: Winston Morgan

Produced in association with The Maxine Co-Op.

Act One

(Lights up on NOELLE, facing the audience.)

NOELLE: Somebody told me, start with a joke. I'm not good with jokes. I know some, there's been funny things happen to me, but they're not like jokes. (My brother Chris is in AA.) He stays away from me. I guess I'm a bad influence on him. This girl fucked Chris when her boyfriend was out of town. The boyfriend comes back, a little while later they've both got the clap. So she goes to Chris and takes him to the clinic. The clinic says Chris doesn't have the clap. This girl wouldn't believe it. See, she knows her boyfriend didn't fuck her over when he was out of town, she must have got it off Chris, except Chris doesn't have the clap. She got this dirty disease and she must have got it off dirty Chris, right? The almost exact same thing happened to me.

Anyway, he's in AA, Chris. I know about this kind of place, I've heard about meetings, it isn't a new idea to me. I'm a bad influence on my brother. Maybe he thinks he caught it off me.

There was one time, Mother's Day. Martin took me out for dinner. We had probably five hundred dollars with us, more, but Martin has to use this credit card that we'd been using way too long already. I said, let's pay cash, but he hands over the card. Well, the guy stalls us, keeps us there, says the computer's fucked up, all that, I said to Martin, they called the cops. Anyway, make a long story short Martin had to stab the waiter. Oh, man, we're outside, running, I'm wearing this dress I've got to hold up, heels on, skipping through all these puddles.

That isn't actually a joke, I guess. Maybe you had to be there. Martin and I had some laughs.

Jerry and his girlfriend, Sheila, Sheila wasn't her name, I'd see her downtown, I didn't know her. We didn't need partners, but Martin cut Jerry in and there wasn't anything I could say about it. So Jerry and Sheila were partners with us. Jerry had dope. I mean he had armloads of dope, bags of it, it never ran out and, naturally, that's why Martin hooked up with him. Listen. They went out every day, they came back with three or four thousand dollars, Jerry lay the money out on the bed. All of it was in hundreds. I told them they should be careful changing all the money to hundreds, the bank remembers it. Well, they didn't go to the bank. Martin is out all day steering, making calls, setting things up and Jerry sits in the bar and does the actual dealing. He does deals Martin never sees. I said, guys buy off Jerry all day and every one of them pays in hundreds? Think about it. Martin doesn't want to think about it.

They buy an ounce, a couple of ounces, cap it up and there's like a baggie of it that we shoot. A baggie. Just scoop it out of the bag. Needle jams, fuck it, fire it into the carpet. Scoop out some more. There's dope on the dresser, in the carpet, a nightmare of junk and nobody worries about heat except me. Every day Jerry buys a couple ounces and he pays with hundreds. New hundreds. Every night they come back and they count out all their hundred dollar bills.

You understand what was happening? All this money, all these new hundreds. It's marked money.

Martin isn't stupid. It was the situation, it made him that way. It made him want to not think. I knew what was going on, I stayed in it, that isn't too bright either. I said to him, let's just grab a bag of it, start on our own, we could have a nice business for ourselves. Well, you can imagine. Martin doesn't fuck over a partner. I only mentioned it once.

Jerry buys an ounce off a guy, pays him with marked money. It's proof the guy sold to them. Jerry would testify he bought six ounces off this guy, three off that guy, the hundreds he paid with prove it. Now, Jerry never testified.

The night we got pinched, the cops shot Jerry, killed him, that was that. Sheila and I got hooked with the dope and then we all sat there waiting, hours and hours, me, Sheila and the cops. Waiting for Martin. They would have killed him, but Martin never showed up. They had fuck all on him, nothing. All they could do was shoot him and he didn't show. So that's how I got pinched.

That's what happened to me. I'm here, it isn't my idea. Somebody said, that chick that got up the other day, she said she looked back on her life and it was a black hole. Well, okay. I look back and it's, I guess all I can say about it, I miss Martin. That's about it. I miss Martin.

(Blackout.)

(Lights up on NOELLE, talking on the telephone in her apartment.)

NOELLE: I don't get it, what are you saying? You know this, this is a fact? Well, how long has he been dead?

Hey, fuck you, I knew him, too. You're nothing special.

(She looks in her address book and dials another number. There is a knocking at the door and she opens it with the phone to her ear. CHRIS enters, carrying a knapsack or suitcase. NOELLE is frozen, seeing him.)

Hello, Peter? Hold the line.

(She covers the mouthpiece.)

You got any money?

CHRIS: What do you mean?

NOELLE: Money. Do you have any?

CHRIS: Well I, not much.

(NOELLE speaks into the phone. While she talks she returns to her original position and CHRIS closes the door behind him.)

NOELLE: Peter, it's Noelle. Yeah, well, they're not good. I've got a situation here, this thing, I need a guy in like an hour. Not violence. Keep guessing. No. No, I can't. My brother just got here, he's right here. That's it. Tried him, he's naturally the first person I thought of and I just can't get hold of him. Did you know that Ronnie is dead? Yeah, I talked to his wife. Who does she think she's kidding? Well, come on, man, how about you? It's just a little show. Five. I was thinking, three for me because I'm setting it up, right? Can we fight about it later? Peter, this would be like a real favour to me. Don't call me back, the guy's going to be here in an hour, what's the point calling me back? I don't see your problem with this. Look, we'll split it, two and a half each, what about that? I said, what if we split it?

(NOELLE listens for a moment and hangs up.)

Stoned. Nodding out right on the phone and I didn't even get it. I'm losing my touch, Chris. What do you want?

CHRIS: I know you're angry with me and I don't blame you. What do I want? Everybody asks me that, I never know how to answer. Denise, I told her how I felt, it was obvious I wanted to get out of there, move out, end it. And she kept saying, what do you want? Actually, what she really said was I didn't know what I wanted. That's one they like to say. You don't know what you want. Do you mean for breakfast? Do you mean I don't know if I want to take a shower or read a book? What I want for the rest of my life? It's one of those questions, it's bullshit.

NOELLE: What do you want?

(CHRIS opens his bag and takes out a stuffed animal. He offers it to NOELLE, who just stares at it.)

CHRIS: I want to give you this. Doesn't it remind you of the one you had on Mill Street? Take it. That's the first thing I want.

NOELLE: Chris, I hope you're joking, I really do. I need money, honey. What have you got?

CHRIS: Don't be like that. I brought you a little present. It's been a long time.

NOELLE: Golly, it's like a prize at the fair. Remember the fair we never went to and the stuffed animal you never won for me? It really takes me back. How much did you come with, a couple hundred? More, I'll bet.

CHRIS: Everything, it all happened at once with me. I didn't have any money, I had to leave. It was like that, all of a sudden. It was, you know what it was like? Arson. I was there, like a warehouse full of broken toasters, I'm drenched in gasoline. One match, boom, everything went up in flames at the same time. No sparks, no smouldering, just boom.

NOELLE: Money. How much?

CHRIS: Denise paid for the ticket.

NOELLE: Stop it.

CHRIS: Fifty bucks. A little less than that.

NOELLE: Hello? It's what? Where does she think you'll stay, in a tree house? Call Denise right now. You need money.

CHRIS: She paid for the ticket. I can't ask her for any more money. We broke up. You know one thing I found out?

NOELLE: Call her, tell her breaking up was a mistake. You're thinking it over. You want to get your head together, maybe go back and try it again. It could happen. It isn't actually lying.

CHRIS: One thing I found out, there's things I can live with and things I can't. I've heard people, they couldn't live if they stole, committed adultery, told lies. I've done all those things. The thing that does me in, I can't live with it, is hypocrisy.

NOELLE: Tell her you might be back there next week. You need money.

CHRIS: You're not listening to me. I just got off the plane, what the hell is this?

NOELLE: Don't get up on your hind legs, man. Just don't. It's a cute trick, but it took you too long to learn it. Ten fucking years, I'm supposed to weep, you want me to fall down and kiss your boots? Ten years wasn't my idea. Fuck you, Chris. You're here, I need money, you're going to get me some. You don't call Denise, call someone else.

CHRIS: I'd like, could I please have a cup of coffee? (Let's have a coffee and calm down and talk about this.)

NOELLE: There's a guy going to be here in an hour, not even that (I owe him money and I've got to have it. Five hundred. Three, really.)

CHRIS: Can't you just go out?

NOELLE: Yeah, but I can't stay out. Grow up.

CHRIS: Well, I don't have it. Sorry, but I don't.

NOELLE: Put your hands up. If I find more than fifty bucks on you, I keep it. Deal?

CHRILS: You're not going to frisk me. It's outrageous.

NOELLE: What do you care if you're telling the truth?

(CHRIS holds out the stuffed animal and speaks as though it's the animal talking.)

CHRIS: It's not nice to call your brother a liar.

(NOELLE punches the animal out of his hand and across the room.)

That's mean, Noelle.

(NOELLE picks up the phone, looks up a number in her book, and dials.)

NOELLE: It's Noelle Terry calling for Angelo. Ang, if you get this message in the next, I don't know, half hour or twenty minutes, shit, there's no time, man. Forget it. *(She hangs up.)* You must have friends. Don't they have jobs? It isn't that much money. Look, call three people, ask them to send a hundred each. A hundred is nothing. Three hundred, ten years, its thirty dollars a year. Ten birthdays, ten Christmas presents, that's twenty, fifteen bucks a year. Fifteen fucking dollars a year, Chris, it's nothing, you owe it to me. Call your friends, get me three, get me two hundred, what about that? Ten lousy bucks for every year I didn't hear from you (You were out here twice, everybody saw you but me. You know what a fucking idiot I looked like?) You call some people.

CHRIS: I can't do it. I wouldn't be here with fifty dollars if I could've got more. What is this guy going to do, kill you? I mean, can't he wait?

(A pause while they watch one another.)

NOELLE: You want a coffee?

CHRIS: That'd be great.

(NOELLE goes to an automatic coffee-maker set up on a table in the corner of the room and does the necessary things.)

I was going to phone, I was going to write, I just didn't. When I was here before I was going to see you and I just kept putting it off. Actually, it's funny. I always thought if I called you, the first thing you'd want would be money. Anyway, that doesn't matter. I left Denise, I'm not moving to England, I'm here. This is, how long have you lived here?

NOELLE: Since I got out.

CHRIS: Sure. Of course. Nice place.

NOELLE: Don't be stupid. Are you going to hug me or something?

(CHRIS goes to her and they have an awkward hug.)

You been lifting weights? You feel like you just got out of the joint.

CHRIS: Yeah, I've got weights at home. She'll probably sell them, I guess.

NOELLE: You didn't join the Y, start playing handball, maybe a little tennis?

CHRIS: Why, because I'm sober? Is that what you think we do?

NOELLE: Yep.

CHRIS: Yeah, well, I actually went to the fucking Y once, you're right. I couldn't cut it.

NOELLE: I just wondered if you were still my brother.

CHRIS: I don't think the Y would change that. Or tennis or golf or anything else.

NOELLE: Well, man, something did.

CHRIS: Noelle.

NOELLE: You know who I ran into? Dean. He asked about you. He was lugging this gym bag, it was big enough to steal watermelons. A regular little athlete.

CHRIS: Dean. He must be what now, fifty?

NOELLE: Looked great. I told him you were married again, someone I don't know, never even seen a picture of. You tell her any of that, what's her name, Denise? You and Dean?

CHRIS: She knows my past, I know hers. I met her in AA. She doesn't care.

NOELLE: She didn't care you were with him? Unusual woman.

CHRIS: It's in the past. I haven't done anything like that since I stopped drinking.

NOELLE: You weren't drunk when you met Dean.

CHRIS: Drugs, same thing. Maybe I wasn't actually stoned the day I met him, you know, but it was that period in my life. That whole time in my life, it's a way of thinking. I changed that. Are you happy to see me? Do you feel okay about it? Is this weird?

NOELLE: I don't know how I feel about it.

CHRIS: My life is fucked. Almost everything anybody says about anything is wrong. It's unbelievable. Snowflakes, it drove me crazy, I think it started with snowflakes. We're all different, unique, right, like fucking snowflakes, no two alike. I heard it once too many times. I thought, it's snowing in Toronto, on Baffin Island, in Mongolia. *None* of them match? Who says? I realized that *most* snowflakes are alike, not none of them.

You ever think about killing yourself? I thought, look, it takes more guts to stay alive than it does to kill yourself.

See, it's like the snowflakes. *Who says? Does* it take more guts to live, do I believe it? The idea was already living in my head, I didn't even have to think it. You have thoughts, I do, that are like bad neighbours, you know, neighbours who make a lot of noise but you just put up with them.

That's my mind, that's what lives in there. Bad neighbours.

NOELLE: I can't believe you haven't been with another guy since Dean. Not even a little bit. You were really into that, him, the whole scene.

CHRIS: I'm sober now. I'm not saying, I mean, I'm a flirt. I can be. I've committed most sins in my heart. I don't mean to say it's a sin. What are we talking about?

NOELLE: True love. You and Dean living together.

CHRIS: I was hiding out then, right? I needed a safe place. I mean, that was part of it. Fucking Dean. Ripped to the tits every day on pot and self-righteous as hell, he was so fucking, I don't even want to talk about it. It makes you feel any better, I've never looked Dean up, either.

NOELLE: It never bothered me, you and Dean. It seemed right.

CHRIS: Listen, I'm assuming, I mean I'm just assuming you don't want to talk about the bit you did.

NOELLE: It would have been nice getting a letter, then. You've never done any time, right? What have you done, a week-end?

CHRIS: I want to make it up to you, Noelle.

NOELLE: Well that's good to hear, because I need you to help me.

CHRIS: My life just changed on me and I couldn't bring you into it. Now it's changed again.

NOELLE: I want you to fuck this guy with me.

(Pause.)

CHRIS: Fuck him up?

NOELLE: No, just fuck him. He's going to be here in, like, forty-five minutes. Listen to me. I need money, I called this guy, I haven't seen him for a couple of years. He wants two of us, me and a guy, he'll pay five hundred bucks. I've done this before, with him. Usually, he just likes to watch, but it's an anything goes situation. You understand? I'm sure he'll settle for the two of us on him. I know it.

CHRIS: You need this money to pay this other guy back? They're both coming here?

NOELLE: There is no other guy, I made it up. That was a lie. This guy will pay me five hundred. I can't find anyone who'll do it with me. Fucking Ronnie is dead. I figured if you could give me the five, I'd cancel the date. If you gave me three I'd cancel, I'd have to give two to whoever I did it with, anyway. If you won't give me the money, I've got to do this guy. I need a partner.

CHRIS: Holy shit.

NOELLE: I'll give you two hundred. You need the money.

CHRIS: What's the five hundred for, the three hundred? Why do you need it?

NOELLE: I don't need three hundred. I could use, I want maybe a hundred bucks. But this guy is offering five hundred. If that's what I'm turning down, I've got to get that back from somewhere. Right? I can't turn down five and take a hundred. I'm losing money.

CHRIS: Noelle, shit. Ten years. Why do you have to, why is this fucking happening? Jesus.

NOELLE: Will you quit talking about ten, I know it's ten years. Will you shut up about it? I didn't invite you here. Not even a fucking letter in the joint, I was doing my bit, not word one. You have to do this for me. You have to do it.

CHRIS: You have to, you have to.

NOELLE: No, I don't.

CHRIS: This is, you don't even care, it doesn't matter to you what's happening to me.

NOELLE: Oh, fuck you. You've been a complete asshole. Don't start making speeches about caring. Save it for your group.

CHRIS: You need a hundred dollars. You call this guy up and he offers you five hundred for sex. Sex with you and another man. Now you think you have to have five hundred because that's what this guy offered you. It doesn't even make sense. You walk into a bank with a cheque for twenty dollars. They cash it, open up the drawer and there's like two grand in there. What do you think, you should get two thousand instead of the twenty just because it's there?

NOELLE: That's right. That is correct. That is what I'm told by those noisy little neighbours in my head. You fuck, you fucker, you fucking asshole. Don't talk like that to me again, Chris.

CHRIS: The day I moved, the last time I moved when I lived out here, you showed up with that guy you ripped off. I shook his hand, I talked like a fool for ten minutes about moving, finally you told me he was there to get money. You brought him to my place and if I didn't have money we were going to have to beat him up, throw him out, he knows where I live. Day fucking one and already I was living somewhere I didn't want to be anymore. So this is nothing new. This is something you live in and it never ends.

NOELLE: Get the fuck out of here.

CHRIS: My pleasure.

(*He picks up his bag and gets as far as the door. Turns to her and puts the bag down.*)

Oh, Noelle, let's not do it again. I don't want this anymore.

NOELLE: I told you, take your fucking, get your, you think I'm kidding?

(*She grabs his bag and tries to open the door to throw it out into the hall. CHRIS leans against the door and reaches for her. NOELLE punches and kicks and CHRIS wrestles with her. The struggle takes them from one side of the room to the other and by the time CHRIS wrestles NOELLE to the floor, his shirt has been ripped almost off his back and he's popped all the buttons off NOELLE's blouse. He straddles her, holding her arms down by the wrists, no different from when they were kids. NOELLE begins to cry. CHRIS quickly gets to his feet and helps her up. She sobs against his chest and they stand in close embrace.)*

CHRIS: Can I please have a cup of coffee?

NOELLE: Shut up.

(She kisses him softly on the mouth, not deeply but not sisterly.)

NOELLE: He'd probably pay five hundred to watch us fight. If you tore the rest of my clothes off.

CHRIS: I don't like fighting with you.

NOELLE: I'm glad you're here, Chris.

CHRIS: What are we going to do?

NOELLE: What do you want to do?

CHRIS: I mean, I mean, I mean about the guy. This guy, the money guy.

NOELLE: Well, you know, what can we do? You know the situation.

CHRIS: I'd, you know, I don't know.

NOELLE: You'd like a cup of coffee.

CHRIS: I really would.

(NOELLE lets go of him, goes to the machine and pours them each a cup.)

CHRIS: I take it black.

NOELLE: I know.

CHRIS: Maybe you should put on another shirt. Aren't you cold? Maybe a sweater.

NOELLE: Are you cold?

CHRIS: No.

(He opens his bag, finds a shirt and puts it on.)

Denise always gives me a hard time about clothes. She thinks I'm too drab. She buys shirts for me but I never wear them. They make me feel conspicuous.

NOELLE: You're not interested in Dean, you're not interested in guys at all. You're not interested in money. How do you feel about junk?

CHRIS: That's what this is all about, isn't it?

NOELLE: The opiate of the masses.

CHRIS: You must know how I feel. Why even talk about it? I'm not going to argue. I don't even want to explain it.

NOELLE: I've been clean almost three months. Part of my parole, I have to go to the fucking meetings.

CHRIS: Holy shit.

NOELLE: Yeah. I've been going and getting somebody to sign my sheet for me. Lately I've been signing it myself.

CHRIS: Three months. You must have already heard it, but why not try one more day?

NOELLE: Because this is the day I want it. Today. The only day of the week I worry about.

CHRIS: If you really wanted junk, you've really made up your mind, you wouldn't be telling me this.

NOELLE: I'm telling you I've tried meetings. I gave them a shot, so you don't have to try and save me. Those people, I don't how you do it. They're scared, like scared little kids, they want bad things not to happen. If you don't follow the program you get cancer. They think, they say their prayers and they're good boys and girls, nothing bad will happen. Anything bad does happen, like to somebody else especially, they figure out where he went wrong, how it can't happen to them. They think they'll live forever. Do you believe that shit? Are you still my brother?

CHRIS: It beats heroin.

NOELLE: What does?

(Pause.)

CHRIS: I used to pray every night that you'd find the program, you'd come to meetings. Okay, sure, I can see where you'd have problems. We all do. The first time you see the signs at the front of the room, the slogans, it's bad news. There's these clichés, one day at a time, keep it simple, easy does it. What the fuck am I doing here? It's easy to think you're too smart for it. But let me tell you, you think they're clichés, but let me tell you. *(Pause.)* Well, they are clichés. That's a fact. I had a sponsor, I got rid of him, I haven't had one in years, but this guy said, there's a reason clichés have become clichés. Right? He's saying they're true, they've lasted through time, that's how they became clichés. I felt better. And then, all of a sudden, I didn't feel better any more. They've been around a long time, it means fuck all. Santa Claus has been around a long time. Neckties have been around a long time, and there is nothing more useless than a fucking necktie. Clichés, you believe them, you become one. A cliché is, it's like a necktie. It's the necktie you hang yourself with in your cell. God damn it, I'm writing that down. I can never think of those things at the time. Listen. The thing is, you can stop using drugs. It'll work. It shouldn't work, but it does. Because of God. I was supposed to go to England. They accepted me at a theological school in Nottingham. Did the old man tell you?

NOELLE: I figured it was bullshit. You were trying to beat him for the tuition money.

CHRIS: No. No. It's, I don't know what to say. It's a long story.

NOELLE: He isn't interested if it's just me. I should have set up a partner first. I was greedy. Fucking Ronnie.

CHRIS: It takes more guts to live than to kill yourself. That's what I was thinking without even thinking. Obviously it's, just look at it. It's always harder to do something new than just to keep on going. Basic law of physics. You only hear that it takes more guts to go on living from people who don't want to kill themselves. They have guts. Makes it kind of self-serving.

NOELLE: It's television talk, that's all.

CHRIS: Christ, Denise and I watched a lot of TV.

NOELLE: It's a married thing.

CHRIS: I'm supposed to know what to say to you and I don't. I'm not going to kill myself. That's not what I'm talking about. I don't think, this guy, I'm not ready for it.

NOELLE: Just take it out of your pants and close your eyes. Two-fifty each.

CHRIS: Shit, it's been, how old is the guy? What does he look like? Do I look kind of heavy to you?

NOELLE: Do you want to just watch? He might go for it.

CHRIS: Is he young?

NOELLE: No younger than we are. You look great, Chris. You feel great.

CHRIS: See, this is the kind of thing, this is why, Noelle, I'm not kidding, you scare me. This fucking guy, you know, I was going to be a priest.

NOELLE: Anglican. You can still have sex.

CHRIS: I'd have to think, I have to think about it. Why does it have to be tonight? Why right now?

NOELLE: It's like this, we fuck the guy. Make him kneel down, pull down your pants, close your eyes. Or else sit down, don't say anything, just look at us. Don't smile. I'll tell him you're a cop, a vice cop, you're forcing me to do this. He'll like that one, I'll bet. Okay. All that's left, you could do something to me or I do something to you and that's out, right? We're not doing this tomorrow or next week or at midnight. We're going to do it now. So what's it going to be?

CHRIS: I'm going to phone the old man and ask him for two-fifty. He won't like it, but he'll do it. It isn't fair to him, he doesn't have money.

NOELLE: Call him now.

CHRIS: I just got off the fucking plane.

NOELLE: Call him now, because I'm not sending my guy away and then find out you can't get the money.

(The phone rings and NOELLE snatches it up.)

Go. Who the fuck is No-elle? Nobody here by that name. It's *Nole*, like stole, like hole, you know? *(She laughs.)* It's a little joke, what do you think it is? The right way to say it is any way you want to say it, I was just teasing you, bad man. There's someone here and we're just talking about you. Well, you'll have to see for yourself. Just when is that going to be, sugar? *(Pause.)* Hold the line.

> *(NOELLE covers the mouthpiece with her hand and goes to CHRIS as though to whisper something to him. CHRIS meets her halfway and NOELLE licks his upper chest, where the shirt is open. It is a long, upward lick, like a cat cleaning a kitten. She puts the phone back to her mouth.)*

He can wait, but not forever. The sooner you're here, the quicker you'll know. Don't make us start without you.

(She hangs up.)

Okay, he's going to be late. Not too late, he's scared of fucking this up, I'm such a busy girl. We've got a little time to hunt around here and find you a pair of balls, a good set of balls that swing. The kind that men have.

CHRIS: You said you'd done it with him before, he doesn't even know how to say your name. You don't know him, do you?

NOELLE: The customer is always right, I don't correct them. I don't know him that well, but I know him.

CHRIS: I know this sounds, it'll sound, you think, listen to me, Noelle. There is a God. I'm saying it. There is a God. I said it.

NOELLE: You'd make the blind see, brother. You really would.

CHRIS: I'm not kidding. I'd be nowhere without God.

NOELLE: You're in my room. You fucked up your marriage and you've got fifty bucks. I was you, I'd give the Devil some serious consideration.

CHRIS: Noelle, I do this thing I *am* the Devil.

NOELLE: You can just watch, I said. Or pull down your pants and don't watch. Will a blow job send you to Hell?

CHRIS: It's helping you get drugs. It doesn't matter how I help.

NOELLE: You're helping me get money. I need money. Your sister is fucking broke and after ten years, not a word and not a dime, you won't, you stand there, you're being a smug little cocksucker. Ex-cocksucker. Reformed whores are worse than anybody. Look at you. I need you to help me and you are going to fucking help me. All you have to do is sit still and shut up. That isn't a whole lot to ask. How I spend my money is my own fucking business. You understand? My money, my business. You understand?

CHRIS: You're right. I understand.

NOELLE: You want some more coffee?

CHRIS: Maybe half a cup. I'm a little jumpy.

NOELLE: You'll be fine.

(NOELLE refills his cup, etc.)

CHRIS: Have you ever thought about this before? With me?

NOELLE: This situation? No.

CHRIS: Have you ever thought about having sex with me?

NOELLE: I'm not asking you to have sex with me, Chris.

CHRIS: But what I'm saying is, have you ever thought about it? At all. In any way.

NOELLE: Well, for a couple of years, on and off, I thought about tracking you down in Toronto and getting somebody to break your thumbs. Martin knows plenty of guys who'd do that. Cheap, too. Then I started getting quite angry at you. I thought about putting you in a wheelchair for life or maybe having you blinded. It's a lot more expensive, but you get what you pay for. Then I just thought about having you killed. I probably haven't thought about it for a year. Maybe once or twice. But, really, the last year or so I haven't thought much about you at all. So no. I didn't think about fucking you.

CHRIS: All I have to do is walk out of here, leave, that's the end of it. You can't stop me. I don't have to be here when the guy comes. What were you going to do, anyway? You didn't know I'd show up.

NOELLE: You leave and I'm fucked. You happy? But where are you going to go with fifty bucks? Dean's?

CHRIS: I'm just saying.

NOELLE: Okay. You said. You've got about oh, no time to make up your mind.

CHRIS: He's going to be late.

NOELLE: We're not going to be drinking coffee when he walks in. This guy's paying five bills.

CHRIS: What's his name?

NOELLE: Lewis.

CHRIS: Lewis.

(NOELLE changes her clothes. She does it without haste and her options are many. The main point of the exercise is that she spend the bulk of her time partially naked—or naked—in front of her brother. She strips down to her underwear while she hunts through her clothes for the appropriate outfit. She can wear skimpy underwear, she can be topless, she can be wearing a halfslip and a G-string. Whatever.

She will not get into garter-belt and stockings or leather gear. (Whatever she changes into makes the actress look devastating.) NOELLE's disrobing and dressing will take place until the end of the act. It's a low-rent Dance of the Seven Veils.)

There's a charter flight going from Miami to Rome. The plane is full, they've been in the air about three hours when the pilot makes an announcement. He says, there's good news and bad news.

NOELLE: This is a joke?

CHRIS: Yes. There's good news and bad news. The bad news is, I've got no idea where the hell we are. The good news is we're making damn good time. *(Pause.)* I think that pretty much says it. *(Pause.)* The slogan, but for the Grace of God, you hear everyone fuck it up. The grace of God, it sounds like bullshit to you, but it's the whole thing. I don't think grace comes and comes and comes. You can say no to it. What always bothered me, I believe in the grace of God, I'm sober and clean and alive by God's grace, but what does it mean if somebody can't get sober, can't stop using? I've got the grace of God, but they haven't? See, I think you can say no to it.

NOELLE: This is the kind of shit that worries Dad. He said to me, can you imagine Chris going for this religion thing? I said, Chris has been a religious maniac all his life. When I was in grade three or four you wanted to die on a fucking cross. You told me that's how you wanted to die.

CHRIS: I was in the fifth grade. It was just kid's talk.

NOELLE: It isn't as common as you think. It's not like wanting to be a fireman.

CHRIS: I got sober by the grace of God. I'm sober today by God's grace.

NOELLE: It beats dying on the cross. Good for you, Chris.

CHRIS: Oh, fuck, Noelle, I can't tell you what to do. I said no. I was supposed to be a priest and I said no. I'm here not because God sent me. Lewis isn't coming over because of God. This is about saying no.

NOELLE: The joint changes your body. You get thick or something. I start feeling like an old house cat. Would you pay five hundred for this? If you weren't my brother?

CHRIS: I am your brother.

NOELLE: Try to imagine you're not.

CHRIS: I'm tired imagining. I was worn out being a priest before it even started. You know what you are, it's bad enough. Bad enough without imagining.

NOELLE: I'm trying to remember the body I had. Not imagine it. Remember. You remember it?

CHRIS: No.

NOELLE: No? You don't remember? Come on. I had a great fucking body.

CHRIS: I can imagine.

NOELLE: You think I look that bad, now?

CHRIS: No.

NOELLE: Don't overwhelm me with compliments.

CHRIS: I'm your brother.

NOELLE: Yeah, okay. Yeah. When he gets here, Lewis, you're not my brother.

CHRIS: What do you want me to do, join the Y?

NOELLE: Should I shave my legs? They're not really smooth, but I don't think they're rough. Are they rough?

(CHRIS doesn't touch her leg.)

CHRIS: Call Lewis and tell him not to come.

NOELLE: Are you going to give me five hundred dollars?

CHRIS: Yes.

NOELLE: Yes?

CHRIS: I've got, never mind how much I've got. More than five hundred, but not a lot more.

NOELLE: I don't believe you. Let me see it.

(NOELLE follows CHRIS to his bag. He pulls an envelope out of the bottom and counts out five bills—half the money. He puts the other five back into the envelope, begins to put it back into the bag, then thinks better of it and sticks it in his pants pocket. CHRIS hands the five hundred-dollar bills to NOELLE.)

New hundreds. They still make me want to scream.

CHRIS: It's real money. Call Lewis and tell him to forget it.

NOELLE: He's on his way, I'll have to tell him when he gets here. Man, you really don't want to do this thing, do you? His five only gets him an hour and it won't even take that. Five from him, this five, five more in your pants. It's a decent amount of money, Chris.

CHRIS: I'm giving you this so he stays out of it. You don't like it, give it back.

NOELLE: Fifty bucks. Did God show you how to lie?

CHRIS: God isn't in this.

NOELLE: You gave me this, it's mine, you have no say in what I do with it. I hope you're straight on that.

CHRIS: I'm not giving it to you. It isn't a gift. I'm paying you.

NOELLE: For what?

CHRIS: For sex.

(Pause.)

Fuck it, forget it, I didn't mean it.

(He reaches for the money and NOELLE keeps it from him.)

NOELLE: Whoa, whoa. You already paid the girl, big guy. You change your mind, you don't get a refund.

CHRIS: You tell Dad, I'll deny it. He knows you're crazy.

NOELLE: I'm crazy? You've got the balls to say that?

CHRIS: Give me my money. I can take it from you if I have to.

NOELLE: Maybe. It sure won't take much to tear off my clothes this time. Go ahead, Chris.

CHRIS: All right, listen. I'm okay. The money, fuck it. There. I gave it to you. I can't stop you using drugs, at least I can stop you turning tricks. I'm giving you that money, it's half of everything I have, I'm bailing you out of the situation with Lewis. The only thing I'd like, tomorrow come to a meeting with me. This is, this situation, it's, this could be the grace of God entering your life. There's a woman, a woman about your age at my home group.

NOELLE: Hush. We can do it. You want to do it with me, we can do it. I'll do it.

CHRIS: You must think I'm really fucked up.

NOELLE: You know what you want. A lot of people don't.

CHRIS: Why the hell don't I want a new car, or a boat or a house? Other guys do.

NOELLE: You know what you want. Don't you?

CHRIS: I want, if we did it, I want, I don't want kissing and hugging or anything else. You know? We're only going to do it once and I want to do it to death.

NOELLE: I'll do anything.

CHRIS: Jesus Christ, Noelle.

NOELLE: But we're going to wait for Lewis. Just a second. I can't just do it. I mean, can you do it? Just like this? Could you take off your clothes right now and do it?

CHRIS: Yes.

NOELLE: If he's here, okay, it's something we do. I understand that. I can understand the shape of it. And there's, we can really do it, you know? There's nothing we can't do in front of Lewis, the badder the better. He isn't paying to watch romance. I can do it with Lewis, but I can't do it without him.

CHRIS: Money. It's all you're about. You have to have that extra five hundred from him, just because it's there.

(NOELLE folds the five hundreds in half and shoves them down the front of CHRIS's pants. She keeps her hand there while she gives him a long, deep kiss on the mouth. When she pulls her hand out, it's empty.)

NOELLE: Too bad you don't like kissing. You're good at it.

CHRIS: I don't know if I can do it. I've thought about this a long time. Somebody watching, I don't know. It makes it weirder. I already feel pretty fucking weird.

NOELLE: It makes it normal. He watches, he pays, I can understand it. You'll like Lewis, he doesn't act stupid. He doesn't breathe through his mouth and he doesn't say all that bad shit. He's kinky, he's

	very, very kinky, but he just does it, you know. He does it and that's all. You'll like him.
CHRIS:	You have to help me.
	(NOELLE reaches under the dresser and pulls out a plastic bag. She takes a cheap pair of handcuffs from the paraphernalia and leaves the bag on top of the dresser.)
	You should get this place painted, I could do it for you. I've been painting, I'm an assistant to this guy, it's an AA thing. That's how I met him, those are mostly the jobs we get, AA people. I don't like it, I don't mean I don't like it, I'm grateful I'm working. See that, I didn't even think it, it's there, that thought. I hate fucking painting. I hate being grateful for things I hate.
NOELLE:	*(Indicating handcuffs.)* Better than rope, cheaper than stockings. Come here.
CHRIS:	No. It's silly.
NOELLE:	Don't make this impossible. You can handcuff me to the bed, maybe tie down my feet. I don't, it isn't something I'd let a trick do, but you, this is okay, it'll be fun. We can do whatever. Lewis will love it. Blindfold me if you want.
CHRIS:	I don't want you blindfolded. I want you in this. You're the whole point.
NOELLE:	What do you want Chris?
CHRIS:	I want everything. I paid you.
	(NOELLE goes to him, takes one of his hands and snaps a cuff on his wrist.)
NOELLE:	Too tight?
CHRIS:	That time in Montreal they nailed me for the gas station, I was handcuffed to a chair all night. They

had me in the basement, my hands were behind my back, they were numb. Those handcuffs have teeth.

NOELLE: I know.

CHRIS: Cops. I don't drink, I don't use, I believe in God. I still hate the fucking cops.

NOELLE: You're still my brother.

(NOELLE leads CHRIS to the bed, but he resists lying down.)

CHRIS: Let's wait for him.

NOELLE: Take your clothes off.

CHRIS: You really should think about getting this place painted. It'd make a world of difference.

NOELLE: I don't want you talking any of this shit when Lewis gets here. He isn't *that* kinky.

(CHRIS pulls off his boots and socks, then takes off his shirt, the handcuffs still dangling from one wrist.)

CHRIS: I'm freezing.

NOELLE: It isn't cold.

CHRIS: My pants, when he gets here, I'll wait. I can take them off or you, later, when you want, open them or pull them down or take them off or something. You use handcuffs a lot? What else is in that bag? I didn't imagine it like this at all. It fucks you up, imagining. It really does.

NOELLE: You don't imagine, what have you got? I mean that's why there's TV. You can't make it up all the time, right?

CHRIS: TV, fuck TV. We should have split up, Denise and I went an extra year because we watched TV.

NOELLE: I'll tell you something, without TV everyone would be a fucking menace. Serial killing would be a hobby. A sport.

CHRIS: You don't have a television.

NOELLE: No. I don't.

> (During this, NOELLE lays CHRIS down on the bed and handcuffs him to the headboard. He lies on his back, his arms above his head. NOELLE quickly finishes changing. The phone rings.)

Go. Oh, Angelo, you're too late, I got somebody. Next time. Well, it was a freak show, you know? Sorry, Ang, the money wasn't that good, anyway. I got a guy, this guy who owes me a lot of favours. Yeah. I knew him a long time ago, then he fucked me over, now he owes me.

> (While she speaks, NOELLE sits on the bed and puts her hand down her brother's pants, pulling out the money one bill at a time.)

I don't have money, Ang, it didn't pay that good. You know how it is, I'm calling everybody and then the right guy comes along, he's just there. Right? God sent him to my door. It's been, I'll tell you, what a fucking day. I called you, it was, did you know Ronnie was dead? Yeah. I was in a corner, I was fucked, and, anyway, it all came together. A fucking miracle. One second and nothing and then, just like that, there's the answer to everything right in my face, right there in front of me. Yep. I just opened my eyes and it was there. There it is.

> (She hangs up the phone.)

End of Act One

Act Two

(Lights up on CHRIS, still handcuffed to the bed. The door is open and NOELLE enters, slamming it shut behind her.)

[handwritten: 3rd choice start]

NOELLE: Your biggest problem? You're stupid. You think too much and you're stupid, it's like the worst combination there is. You have fucked up, you have fucked me out of, you owe me five hundred dollars. I'm out five hundred because you're stupid. This is like paying a fine. My situation, this, it's a crime, being stupid. You get caught and you pay for it. You were always stupid with this stuff, always, always. You were never cut out for it. You owe me money.

CHRIS: Get these fucking things off me.

(NOELLE jumps on the bed, intending to get the rest of the money out of his pocket. CHRIS clamps his legs around her and manages to get his manacled hands on her hair. He holds on with a death grip while NOELLE tries to slug him.)

NOELLE: I'll kill you, I'll fucking kill you, you're making a mistake, Chris. Let me up, you'll die, I'll burn you down, you cocksucker. I'll burn you down to the fucking ground.

CHRIS: Unlock them, take them off me. I'll start screaming.

NOELLE: Go ahead and scream.

(CHRIS screams loudly.)

Jesus Christ. All right, wait don't do it again.

(She unlocks the handcuffs, her hair still prisoner in her brother's hands. Slowly, they disengage and climb off the bed.)

You're a real little girl, Chris.

CHRIS: Your biggest problem, you're a cunt. Right from your lying little mouth to your sagging ass. An ugly little cunt. I gave you half my money for fucking nothing and I don't care how you see it, you're fucked up. You've got five hundred and you didn't do a thing and you're still not happy. Too fucking bad.

NOELLE: You don't tell a guy, you shouldn't have told Lewis you're my brother. It was, it wasn't smart. It's too weird. A guy fucks his sister, maybe he'll kill you later, you know? You don't, I don't think you understand how strange it is. It's really strange to fuck your family, Chris. We're blood.

CHRIS: Oh, fuck you. What do you mean, strange? How can you call anything strange? That guy, that was stupid. Your idea, my fault. Fuck you.

NOELLE: Listen, you, you fucking, you just fucking listen. Five, five, listen. I'm thirty-nine. My ass is as good as anybody's. Sagging ass, that's bullshit. You don't even think that. I'm keeping the money. It's fair. I told you how we had to do it, we had to do it with him, you fucked it up.

CHRIS: Keep it. It's only, keep the fucking money. It's yours.

NOELLE: I did tell you don't tell him, I said that. It's too weird without him. You just don't get that. It's a weird fucking thing to do. Probably you wouldn't even want it if it wasn't me, I mean, if I'm just anybody. If I wasn't your sister, you wouldn't even want to do it.

CHRIS: If you weren't, what, you were someone else I'd spent my whole life with since I was a little boy? You'd be my mother.

NOELLE: I'm not attractive to you. Just as a woman.

CHRIS: It isn't happening, right? It didn't happen. It doesn't matter if you're my sister, my daughter, my goddamned grandmother.

NOELLE: You don't think I'm worth five hundred dollars.

CHRIS: No. I don't. On your own, all by yourself, neither does Lewis.

NOELLE: Nobody would pay you a dime to fuck them.

CHRIS: I know.

NOELLE: Nobody would pay anyone five hundred. Who's worth five hundred?

CHRIS: Madonna.

NOELLE: Okay, besides Madonna.

CHRIS: Well, baby, you're not. That's all that counts right now. It was a fucked up idea. My shrink, I'll figure it out later. I could, I'll show him a picture of Denise, I left Denise. A picture of Molly. They look completely different, blonde, brunette, different bodies. I'll show him a picture of you, a junkie, you just got out, I'll tell him I was going to pay you five bills. He'll probably have me committed, sister or not.

> (*NOELLE throws the handful of wadded-up hundreds in his face. She is too shaken to speak. She walks across the room and throws open the door as though she is about to leave, then steps to the side. It's a clear message for CHRIS to get out. He carefully picks up the bills, smooths them out and walks to the door. He closes it, then offers NOELLE*

the money. She stares at him, no idea what he's doing.)

Could I interest you in some heroin?

NOELLE: One phone call to Martin and you'll be in Stanley Park with your own dick stuck down your throat. Get out of my fucking room.

CHRIS: I need you, Noelle. All I said was, not five hundred. Nobody's worth five hundred. It wasn't personal.

NOELLE: Which one of your multiple personalities am I talking to? You and your shrink laughing at my picture. Sounds personal.

CHRIS: I was pissed off. I gave you five, didn't I? I think you're worth five, I mean, I don't want to put a price tag on you. I was paying for sex, not paying for you. Right? I was mad, I was getting even. I'm sorry.

NOELLE: Now you want to score. Who are you, brother? Ten years you act like a good boy, now you're trying to act like a guy going bad.

CHRIS: Twelve years. It's been ten years since I had a drink. I went bad as soon as I got on the plane, before that, even. As soon as I left Denise. No. As soon as I started sleeping with Molly and I've been sleeping with Molly a long time. I went out, I was, I had sex with a bunch of women. Am I handsome? I'm not handsome, I don't have money, women sleep with me. I could imagine myself in some tiny village in England, some little honey coming to me for advice and two minutes later we're doing it all over the church. The villagers surround the place in the middle of the night holding burning torches. I'm running through the swamp like Boris Karloff, a pack of hungry dogs right on my ass, Denise is crying and the cops are yelling at her. And God, holy shit, God doesn't like it, he doesn't like it a bit.

I'm not going bad, I am bad, I want to be fucking bad. God gave me a chance and I want to be bad instead.

NOELLE: Legally, you're insane. You don't know the difference between right and wrong.

CHRIS: I stopped drinking because I couldn't do what I wanted to do and now I'm sober and I can't do what I want to do. What am I supposed to want? I want to shoot Martin in the knees and cut his throat. I want to live with a woman who doesn't speak English in some other country. I want some junk, I want to fix, I want to shoot a lot of dope.

NOELLE: Don't try to kill Martin, it's a bad idea. Drugs. We need drugs. This, when you quit, this kind of money wouldn't even get us started. Started, maybe, but that's all. Now this pays for a good run. The stuff is so good, they're dying out here like flies. It costs less, you get more.

CHRIS: You've probably heard about the geographical cure. For me, with junk, it worked. In Toronto I don't have connection one. I don't even know where it happens.

NOELLE: You think junk is worth five hundred?

CHRIS: Depends on the junk.

NOELLE: Junk and Madonna.

(She picks up the phone and dials.)

Alex, it's Noelle Terry. Call me. *(Hangs up, dials again.)* Were you still here when Martin shot that guy outside Burger King? Jenny, it's me, call me at home. *(Dials again.)* The guy chased him for a block and, you know, how far is Martin going to run? He starts walking, the guy's still running after him, so Martin shot him. Didn't kill him. *(Into phone.)* You know who this is. Shit. *(Hangs up.)* He gets into another guy's car and makes him drive through a red light, bang, a pick-up hits them, knocks the car right through the front window of a, not the Seven Eleven, that other place. The driver's all smashed up, Martin gets out of the car and robs the till. He goes out, flags down a cab, comes home. Actually not home, he gets out a block away, he's being cautious. Won't pay for the fucking cab, shows the guy the gun and robs him, too. Then Martin comes home and falls asleep. It must have been two hundred cops showed up for him. Anyway, Martin. I keep hearing he wants to kill me. I know Martin's got dope.

CHRIS: Well, shit, what are we waiting for? I mean, run, don't walk.

NOELLE: Are you being funny?

CHRIS: Are you? Martin? Why don't we just stab ourselves and set fire to the money? It saves the trouble of going out.

NOELLE: He doesn't just want to kill me. I've heard that, but he's never said it to me. He gave me a necklace when we were together, he said it was his mother's. I doubt it, but it was nice. He gave it to me Mother's Day. Sometimes he calls me and he says as long as I have the necklace I belong to him. It's just the way he is.

CHRIS: Give it back to him.

NOELLE: I sold it. He has dope.

CHRIS: No. Jesus, Martin. You know what I think of when I think about Martin? I don't, it isn't all the crazy shit he's done. I remember this time, I'd only known him, whatever, not long. We were waiting for a guy, I was nervous, it was some bad news situation. Anyway, Martin is looking in the window of a store, being inconspicuous, right?

Inconspicuous Martin. I can see he's really getting himself worked up and I think it's about the guy we're waiting for, but it isn't. There's a book in the window called *Your Scottish Heritage* and Martin is giving it both eyes. He says, Your Scottish Heritage. I'm not Scottish. And I can see him look in the store and I know he's thinking about going inside and I was fucked. Here's a guy and he's going to get even because there's a book in a window and he isn't Scottish and they're trying to make him feel bad about it. I said, what could I say? Take it easy, man, I said. Martin says, I don't take shit from anybody.

NOELLE: That's him. What you're talking about, I saw him watching a bird in a tree one day and he was giving it that same look. That's the scariest thing about Martin. I thought, he wants to kill all the birds just because he can't fly.

3rd choice to stop

(The phone rings and NOELLE grabs it.)

Go. Oh. Oh, hi. No, that's just the way I answer the phone. Well, you know me, I'm nothing but bad habits. When? I must have been out. I actually haven't been going for a while. Could I call you back? This isn't really a good time to talk. Yes, my brother, he's visiting. Oh, aren't we suspicious. It's my brother. Really. Chris. Well, I do too. Okay. Okay. *(Pause, then she laughs.)* Bye. She hangs up.

NOELLE: Okay, you don't want to try Martin, we can either wait on Alex or hit the street.

CHRIS: Who was that?

NOELLE: Just a guy. I met him at a meeting, we went for coffee a couple of times.

CHRIS: Coffee?

NOELLE: Dark liquid, hot, comes in a cup? We had, I guess, kind of a date. I don't think I ever had a date in my

	life. The meetings, it's like being back in high school, isn't it?
CHRIS:	A date?
NOELLE:	Did you have a stroke while I was on the phone? A date. We went out.
CHRIS:	I don't get it. Why would you go out with this guy?
NOELLE:	You've lost me, babe. What's happening?
CHRIS:	Well, I mean who the fuck is he? Some asshole you run into at a fucking meeting, you don't even like going to them, but this guy, you're having coffee, you're going on fucking dates. You had sex with him, I'll bet, first date.
NOELLE:	Fuck you.
CHRIS:	No, fuck him, you fuck him, not for five hundred, not for five bucks. He probably didn't even pay for your coffee.
NOELLE:	You and him, these are entirely different situations.
CHRIS:	Is he your boyfriend?
NOELLE:	Will you act your age? You want to know if we're going steady?
CHRIS:	Are you?

(NOELLE laughs in utter disbelief.)

Okay, okay, I didn't know you had a guy, a boyfriend. It's a surprise.

NOELLE:	He isn't, listen, he's just a guy. (I slept with him once. I guess twice.)
CHRIS:	You slept with him.
NOELLE:	You have to stop repeating everything I say. He's

not going to show up here, if that's what you're worried about. I don't understand the problem.

CHRIS: No problem. I met Denise, I met Molly at a meeting. This guy, you met him, you went out, he took you home. Right?

NOELLE: More or less.

CHRIS: You went, you had sex with him twice, you must have liked it.

NOELLE: Gee, am I blushing? You got me, reverend. I liked having sex with him, yeah.

CHRIS: He liked it, too. It was probably a whole new experience for him.

NOELLE: It was.

CHRIS: It's normal. People in the program, they get involved all the time. It isn't a good idea, but it happens. I hope he isn't the kind of guy, he snags newcomers, bullshits them, gets them when they're vulnerable. There's a lot of those guys. I guess, really, you stopped using, you went to meetings, you're just the same as everybody else. I'm kind of surprised, maybe I'm a little disappointed, but you're just like any other newcomer. Why not? You meet some dipstick, he feeds you clichés, it sounds like wisdom. I'm thinking, probably he used needles, too, right? You ought to be careful. But you won't be careful. You probably think, the two of you think it's meant to be, you're supposed to fall in love, God's taking care of you. Yeah. I hope you die, Noelle. I hope you get sick and fucking die. I'll see you when you're dead.

(He picks up the money from wherever he put it down and shoves it into his pocket. He puts on his boots.)

NOELLE: What's happening? What the hell happened? Because I fucked him for nothing? You offered the money, I didn't ask for it.

CHRIS: You think everything's about money.

NOELLE: I'm ugly, I've got a fat ass, I don't look like your wife. You said that. You can't promise to fix me and then don't do it. You can't.

CHRIS: Ask your boyfriend.

(NOELLE *grabs a large knife from a box of utensils near the coffee maker. She runs at* CHRIS, *who quickly picks up a chair and threatens her with it.* NOELLE *stops and backs up a step. They circle each other,* NOELLE *lunging in if* CHRIS *tries to pick up his bag or open the door.*)

NOELLE: Why don't you scream?

(*The phone rings when* NOELLE *is next to it and she picks it up.*)

Call back.

(*She begins to hang up, then puts it urgently to her ear.*)

Alex, Alex, don't hang up.

(CHRIS *keeps the chair in one hand and manages to drag his bag over to the door.*)

(*To* CHRIS.) We can score.

(CHRIS *puts down the chair and opens the door.*)

One second, Alex. (*Covers mouthpiece.*) I'll show you what I did with him. On our date. I'll do the same things with you.

CHRIS: Put down the knife.

(NOELLE *throws it across the room.* CHRIS *closes the door and comes back inside.*)

NOELLE: *(Into phone.)* Listen, we're in the market. We've got, like, five. Can you help me out? Name the place, I'm there. I'm at the same place. Alex, I'm here, man.

(She hangs up. Pause.)

Last time I fixed it was right here with Alex. The night before my first meeting. After that, you know, I had a spiritual awakening, turned me a hundred and eighty degrees, blah, blah, blah. He's going to be, he'll be a little while, he picks up in this area. Do you have condoms?

CHRIS: No.

NOELLE: First things first. Hand over that money. You're not going to fuck me out of the dope.

CHRIS: I don't trust you, Noelle.

NOELLE: I don't give a flying fuck, Chris.

(He gives her the money.)

Go and wait in the bathroom.

CHRIS: Is that what you did with him? Is that what he wanted?

NOELLE: No. Is that what you want?

CHRIS: No.

NOELLE: Just go and wait in the bathroom for a minute.

(CHRIS enters the bathroom. While he's there, NOELLE goes to the garbage, removes an empty milk carton and sticks the money into it. She replaces the carton, covering it with garbage. She speaks loudly to CHRIS to cover her movements.)

NOELLE: You like women beating you, Chris?

CHRLS: No.

NOELLE: You like beating them?

CHRIS: No.

NOELLE: Maybe you want a little half and half, a bit of sucking, a bit of fucking. I could just give you head. Or you can go down on me. Whatever.

(CHRIS opens the bathroom door. NOELLE has just finished stashing the money and has stepped away from the garbage.)

CHRIS: What you did with him, you said. You said we'd do the same things. Don't talk to me like I'm a trick.

NOELLE: That's how I talked to him. Charles. I did that the second time, he liked it. You want the first date or the second date? Actually, the second one, you couldn't really call it a date.

CHRIS: Maybe we should wait until we fix.

NOELLE: You won't be any braver. I didn't wait three months so I could blow my fix having sex. (Fixing is fixing and fucking's fucking.)

CHRIS: There's twelve step meetings that are just about fucking. Molly tried that, she wanted us to go together. See, you don't drink, take drugs, smoke, gamble, eat too much or fuck. It's like everyone just got off the Mayflower. Like life is a disease you can recover from. With God.

NOELLE: Are you going to stay in the bathroom?

CHRIS: Okay, we're on a date. We've been out now we're here. Did you come here?

NOELLE: Yes. I'm afraid there's nothing to drink. Would you like to fuck me?

CHRIS: You didn't say that to him.

NOELLE: Oh yes, I did.

CHRIS: I don't want that, I want our date instead. Yours and mine. Later, when it's time, we'll do the things you did with him. Okay?

NOELLE: So it's not me and Charles, it's you and me.

CHRIS: Well, you're you and I'm me, but different.

NOELLE: I'm not your sister?

CHRIS: I want you to be my sister.

NOELLE: Chris, you're a fucking nightmare. You call me up, me, Noelle, and ask me out. We go out together. You, Chris Terry, and me.

CHRIS: We go for dinner. Chinese. After that, we see a movie.

NOELLE: Let's skip the movie. We've had a lot to talk about at dinner, I don't want it to stop.

CHRIS: Right, that's right, good. You like me.

NOELLE: Aha. I like you. I ask you back here and I like you. A lot.

CHRIS: Yes. I like you, too. I hope something will happen.

NOELLE: Yes, sure, because we like each other but we're tense, maybe a little shy. What we really want is to fall into each other's arms.

CHRIS: That's it exactly.

NOELLE: You said you didn't want anything mushy.

CHRIS: Well I changed my fucking mind.

NOELLE: Okay, okay.

CHRIS: You came here with him, Charles, you asked him, you just said it. Then what? You did it?

NOELLE: How much do you want to know? There's no point getting crazy.

CHRIS: He kissed you? Tell me what he did.

NOELLE: I'd already kissed him. Before we got here. He looked sad and I gave him a kiss.

CHRIS: He looked sad. That's a cheap routine. He was hoping you'd mercy fuck him.

NOELLE: Do you want to know or don't you?

CHRIS : Go.

NOELLE: We got here, I asked him if he wanted to fuck me. Not really serious, the same way I said it to you. He laughed, not actually laughed, kind of a smile and he sat me down on his knee.

CHRIS: He's sitting where?

NOELLE: Where you are. He was standing close to me, he took my hand and walked me over. When he sat down, he pulled me onto his lap. He put his arms around me, around my waist, and he put his head on my shoulder. You want to do it?

CHRIS: That isn't what I'd do. I'd lay down with you on the bed.

(He takes NOELLE by the hand and leads her to the bed. He lies down and she stretches out beside him. CHRIS sits up.)

CHRIS: Can you sit up, maybe against here?

(He sticks the pillows against the headboard of the bed and NOELLE sits up straight, her back against them. CHRIS lies on his back his head on her lap.)

Is this good?

NOELLE: I feel like we're waiting for someone to take our photograph.

CHRIS: I like it. It's like being under a tree. I want to

	remember it like this. You sat on his knee, he put his head on your shoulder. Did you talk?
NOELLE:	Yes. I told him, I said, I said things to him. Nice things, things I liked about him.
CHRIS :	Like what?
NOELLE:	No.
CHRIS:	You could say nice things to me. Not the same things. What you like about me.
NOELLE:	You could tell me what you like about me. Charles did.
CHRIS:	That isn't the same. He liked being here, he knew you were going to have sex, I mean he doesn't even know you. He liked the situation.
NOELLE:	What do you like about me, Chris?
CHRIS:	I just met you now? I like your looks, obvious thing. I like the way you walk, how you dress, all of that. I like it you don't care if I like you or not. Your mind is made up, you're not all over the place, running scared. You don't act like anyone else. I like that.
NOELLE:	Charles, what he liked, he told me things about himself. Stuff that happened, how it made him feel. He said he liked me because I didn't have any answers.
CHRIS:	You've got *all* the answers. You know the answer to everything. See, that's first date, first impression. I know you. You *are* the answer.
NOELLE:	What's the question?
CHRIS:	You've got a smart mouth. A bad mouth. I like that, too.
NOELLE:	I was on his knee, his head was on my shoulder. You want to hear about it?

CHRIS: Does it get strange?

NOELLE: Kind of.

CHRIS: You told him the things you liked about him. Then he said the thing about you and answers.

NOELLE: He said that later. He told me some things, he talked about when he first stopped drugs, when he started coming to meetings.

CHRIS: Ho fucking hum. He means, what, like six months ago?

NOELLE: Seven years. Two years ago, I think about two, his guy, the guy Charles talked to, his sponsor, he died. This guy died. Charles is telling me this, not really sad, kind of flat, like a newspaper story. The guy is sick and he dies and he used to be a real genuine bad motherfucker. I mean, a regular Martin. Charles doesn't get into it, but I got the idea. Anyway, one time, I can't remember his name, Charles's sponsor, he's robbing someone on the street. I mean a straight guy, a civilian. He's got some cannon, maybe a .45, right at the guy's head and the guy won't hand over the money. The guy says, you can kill me but you can't make me love you.

CHRIS: Who said it? His sponsor?

NOELLE: No, no, no. Listen. Charles's sponsor, right, he's robbing a businessman on the street. Points a .45 at his head. The businessman says, you can kill me but you can't make me love you.

CHRIS: So?

NOELLE: So nothing. That's the story he told me.

CHRIS: How fascinating.

(NOELLE twists her brother's ear. He reaches up and grabs her arms, but he's in a bad position and

can't do much to stop her. NOELLE gives him an uncomfortable few moments, then stops.)

CHRIS: Jesus, Noelle, that hurts.

NOELLE: Don't you like pain? Everyone likes a little. Especially with your head in my crotch.

CHRIS: Did you twist his fucking ears?

NOELLE: No. He turned me around on his lap so my back was against him. He held me tight, really tight, not around the waist, but a little higher. That was after he told me the story.

CHRIS: Show me.

(They get off the bed and return to their starting point. CHRIS sits and NOELLE straddles his lap, leaning back against him. CHRIS puts his arms around her waist and she raises them so they circle her just beneath the breasts.)

NOELLE: He hugged me tight, tighter than that, then tighter and tighter until I couldn't breathe. Try it.

CHRIS: It sounds stupid. He squeezes you so you can't breathe.

NOELLE: Yes. Then he stopped and I caught my breath. My ribs hurt. I leaned my head back and he kissed my neck. I wanted to turn around and kiss him on the mouth, but he wouldn't let me. He squeezed me again. He just crushed me.

(CHRIS does it. NOELLE moans, squirms slightly, and he relaxes his grip. She takes a deep breath and lets her head fall back on his shoulder. CHRIS kisses her neck.)

He said, he said.

(CHRIS squeezes her again, harder. NOELLE gives a deep groan. He relaxes his grip.)

	He said, he asked me if I felt close to him.
CHRIS:	Did you?
NOELLE:	Yes.

(She begins to stand and CHRIS pulls her back down.)

Let me turn around.

CHRIS:	He didn't let you.
NOELLE:	I turned around, finally. He let me.

(CHRIS releases her. She stands, turns around, straddles his lap facing him. They have their first truly passionate kiss. NOELLE tears open his shirt and pulls it back, exposing a shoulder. She sinks her teeth into the shoulder with great ferocity. CHRIS is just reaching the point where he can't stand the pain when the phone rings. NOELLE jumps off his lap and runs to it. She yanks the receiver to her ear, hearing the dial tone before she gets a chance to utter her famous salutation. She hangs up.)

Martin. He calls and hangs up before he even hears my voice. I think he's afraid a guy will answer and then he'll feel more or less obligated to come over and kill him. He'll call a couple more times and in the middle of the night he'll call for real. I'll ask him did he call before and he'll say no. Martin can do anything in the middle of the night.

CHRIS:	You didn't answer the phone when he was here, did you? Charles.
NOELLE:	What if you woke up at three o'clock in the morning and saw God just standing there. You ask him what he wants and he won't tell you.
CHRIS:	You don't ask God what he wants. You ask the Devil.

NOELLE: If I got up in the morning and I wanted to die, the most interesting way for it to happen, I'd get together with Martin again. He's the only guy who, well that's it right there. He's the only guy. Everybody else, I might as well shoot water. You know when you're sick you'll put some water in there and shoot it, maybe there's a crumb or two inside, a tiny little piece of junk that didn't dissolve? You feel worse, way worse than if you didn't do it at all. You fix and there's nothing in there but water.

CHRIS: Did you bite his shoulder, or were you just biting mine?

NOELLE: I didn't feel so sick after Charles. Usually I just feel sick and I don't know what can fix me. Or what I can fix. I hate the fucking telephone.

CHRIS: Noelle. Noelle, come back to me. The phone didn't ring, you didn't answer, Martin didn't hang up. Okay? You didn't wake up this morning and decide to die.

NOELLE: What?

CHRIS: You didn't decide to die in an interesting way. Not today. Stay away from Martin.

NOELLE: You die anyway.

(NOELLE takes a shopping bag from under the bed and removes half a dozen new, black candles and candleholders from it.)

Help me with these. I want them around the bed.

(CHRIS joins NOELLE and looks inside the bag. He lifts out a black dress and a necklace.)

NOELLE: I'm not wearing that. I don't know what I was thinking of.

CHRIS: This is the necklace Martin gave you? His mother's?

NOELLE: Charles, on our date, our first date, after he squeezed me and squeezed me, he said it was too bright. I lit candles before I got on him again. Before I bit him.

CHRIS: When did you fuck Martin? When's the last time?

NOELLE: You don't want to be on that date, Chris. The last time I fixed, here, with Alex? Martin came over that night.

CHRIS: Here. With Martin. On this bed.

NOELLE: Does it make you shrivel up? Or maybe it makes you hard.

CHRIS: Did you have candles around the bed?

NOELLE: Martin does it in the dark.

CHRIS: That's kind of sweet, really. He's shy, Martin.

NOELLE: The scariest thing Martin ever told me, I asked him why he used a knife when he did a guy. Why not just shoot him? Martin said, I like to touch them. Sometimes I think he goes so far, he fucks up so totally, just so someone will finally touch him.

CHRIS: He's a victim of bad therapy.

NOELLE: Charles doesn't need it to be dark. Charles, he's...

CHRIS: Who the fuck is this guy, Charles? What does he do? For a living?

NOELLE: He paints houses. No, that's you, isn't it?

CHRIS: So what? I was waiting to go to England, go to school. It was fine. I was humble Chris, the happy fucking monk. Then I wasn't going to school, it wasn't going to happen and all I was, I was painting other people's houses. Fuck it.

NOELLE: I got out, they classified me as unemployable. Unemployable and insane. You used to think candles were spooky. You said, when we were in Montreal, you said candles were too much like a bad drug trip.

CHRIS: That was the worst year of my life, except for last year. Probably next year. What I think, what I've always thought, life is a crime. If it wasn't, it wouldn't carry the death penalty. Every cemetery, every tombstone in the world it could say, I fought the law. I fought the law and the law won.

(NOELLE takes the new dress from the bag and puts it on. She hesitates over the necklace, then decides against it.)

NOELLE: We could wait for Alex. It'd be like a dream. You can do it to me, anything you want, we'll be dreaming. I'll just kind of drift away.

(She lies on the bed, surrounded by candles.)

I'll wait until I fix before I put on his necklace. Look at me. How do I look?

CHRIS: You did this shit on your date?

NOELLE: No, no. This is a different game.

CHRIS: I liked the one we were playing. You said you didn't want to wait till we fixed. Are you chickening out?

(NOELLE gets off the bed.)

NOELLE: Okay, sit down. I wore a dress on the date. Not this dress.

(She straddles his lap, facing him.)

I lit the candles and got on him like this and I kissed him. Like we kissed. Then I bit him, same as you, longer. I made him bleed.

CHRIS: Jesus, Noelle. This guy used needles. Don't you understand?

NOELLE: I bit him and I made him bleed. When I took my mouth off his shoulder he put his face close to me. He looked at my mouth and he went, very lightly and very gently, he licked my lips. Just licked them. And he said, blood. Blood.

(She puts her hand on her brother's crotch.)

NOELLE: I unzipped his pants.

CHRIS: Don't do it. Just tell me.

NOELLE: I was holding him in my hand, getting a look at him and he lifted me up by the hips and sat me down, right on top of it. He hooked his thumb in my panties and just moved them over.

(A long kiss between CHRIS and NOELLE.)

CHRIS: Charles is probably hung like a horse, right?

NOELLE: Martin is hung like a horse.

CHRIS: Of course he is. He has to be. If he wasn't, he'd be a pathetic guy running around doing all that shit to make up for the fact he has a small dick and his life would be stupid. Martin is insane, not stupid.

(NOELLE climbs off his lap.)

NOELLE: No, he isn't stupid. I went to jail, Martin didn't. The cops killed Jerry. Where was Martin? He is not stupid.

(CHRIS stands up and pulls her to him.)

Let's get on with this. If you won't wait for Alex, let's do it. I know what you want, but you're not going to admit it.

CHRIS: I know what you're going to say.

NOELLE: You don't want to be Charles on that date…

CHRIS: Wrong, wrong.

NOELLE: You want to be me.

CHRIS: I'm not gay. You can ask my shrink.

NOELLE: You want to be taken by me. Lots of guys want that. I know how to do it.

CHRIS: I'm not gay. Listen, when this is over, my shrink is going to have plenty to say, believe me. I don't think the major issue is going to be about me and guys. This will fuck up his head. Denise, probably she'll never speak to me again. If I tell her. Well, I'll have to tell her. This thing, you and me, it isn't about being gay.

NOELLE: I don't get it.

CHRIS: Well, I'd be here seeing Dean, not you. Right?

NOELLE: What I mean, what are you talking about? You'll tell Denise, your shrink. You're here, that's over.

CHRIS: I don't mean I'll tell them tonight or tomorrow. I mean eventually. When my feet are back on the ground.

NOELLE: When your feet are on the ground.

CHRIS: I'm not going to be a priest. That's pretty much finished.

NOELLE: You're probably right about that.

(NOELLE takes CHRIS by the shoulders and helps him lie down. While she talks, she dumps the contents of the plastic bag onto the bed: collar and leash, leather thongs, a strap, etc. She snaps the handcuffs onto one of his wrists.)

Roll over.

CHRIS: What for?

NOELLE: I've got a surprise and I don't want you looking. Roll over and put your face in the pillow.

(CHRIS does as he's told. NOELLE brings his hands together.)

Relax. I just want your arms out of the way.

(She sticks his hands through the slats on the headboard and snaps the cuffs on his other wrist. CHRIS is handcuffed to the bed, face-down. He tries to free his hands, roll over, etc. and realizes what's happened to him.)

CHRIS: Can we get the surprise over with?

NOELLE: How can you come from the same family as me and be so stupid?

(CHRIS struggles while NOELLE pulls down his pants.)

CHRIS: Okay, okay. I've got no choice. I can't stop you. You can do whatever you want.

NOELLE: You know what happens Chris, what always happens? You say things to me and I actually believe them. After all this time. This is just another little adventure for you, just like everything else. The amazing adventures of Chris.

(NOELLE retrieves the kitchen knife and returns. She stands at the head of the bed so that CHRIS can see her.)

Charles, he liked it with the knife. He didn't say it, naturally, but I finally figured it out. I ran it up between his legs, like I was going to cut his balls off. Oh, he liked it. I cut him a little bit, here and there. I sliced him a little, stabbed him a little. Blood just kind of leaked out of him, not much, nothing to write home about. Then I stuck the point against his Adam's apple and he said, do it. Like that. Do it.

(She holds CHRIS's head up by the hair and moves

the point of the knife over it as though she's writing.)

CHRIS: Keep it away from my eyes. Please, Noelle.

NOELLE: You know something? That girl, she got the clap, she had to tell her boyfriend about you?

CHRIS: I didn't give it to her. She got it off him.

NOELLE: Yeah, that's fine. But she got all the shit, her boyfriend knows she fucked around and he'll never let her forget it. You didn't even get the clap. You got laid, you fucked her up, you got away with it. Story of your life.

CHRIS: I don't want…

NOELLE: No, no, no. What you don't want is over. I don't have a strap-on, I've always meant to buy one. I've got, there's the candle, is it long enough? I don't know what you're used to. Actually, you know, I could call Martin.

(During this, NOELLE goes to the foot of the bed and ties one of the scarves from the bag around her brother's ankle. He struggles in vain while she ties one foot then the other, to opposite corners of the bed.)

Martin's done time. He must have had a boyfriend. I know he thinks that if you're not on the receiving end, you're not queer.

(NOELLE goes to the phone and dials.)

Did you call me and hang up? I just thought it might have been you. Could you come over here, like right now? there's a guy here, well, he's trouble. He's…

(NOELLE waits a second and hangs up.)

You tell him there's trouble, he's here. You guys

haven't seen each other in a long time. It'll be interesting.

(*She pulls the pillow out from under CHRIS's head and shoves it under his groin.*)

I'll save the underwear for him. You're wearing a little something, it can actually be more tempting. You know what I mean?

(*CHRIS says nothing. NOELLE returns to the head of the bed and looks at him.*)

How do you like your movie now?

CHRIS: If it has to happen, if it's going to happen, let it be Martin. Why not?

NOELLE: Don't try that bullshit on me.

CHRIS: I came all the way out here just so I could be Martin's girlfriend. Don't you think that's funny? Watch yourself, Noelle. He might like me better.

NOELLE: You wish.

CHRIS: I understand him. I like his mind.

NOELLE: Don't forget his big dick.

(*NOELLE picks up the plastic bag and pulls it over her brother's head. She keeps it on just long enough to cause him serious panic, then pulls it off.*)

CHRIS: Don't kill me, Noelle.

NOELLE: You fucker. This is what it's like. This is what happens when you don't get away with it.

CHRIS: What do you want from me?

NOELLE: Everyone knows I'm bad. Nobody knows about you. Nobody but me. Why don't you pray? There's a God, pray. You've got God, you don't need anything else. You don't need your sister. God is better than junk, right?

CHRIS: Take the money, all of it. Just take the money and let me go.

(NOELLE takes the money out of his pocket.)

NOELLE: My ad says, very kinky. I started running that ad, I got a few guys, I didn't know what to do with the money. I go shopping. I don't even lift anything, there's no point. Shopping. Then, like today, I need money and it's gone.

CHRIS: You've got money, now. I did this, I'm paying for it. Are you happy?

NOELLE: Do you go shopping, Chris? Do you go to a movie, order a pizza, watch TV? You wake up and you know that's what you'll do that day and it's okay? How do you do that? Like, what is the fucking point?

CHRIS: How the fuck do I know? You think I know? I'm always drowning in shit. Listen, your life isn't my fault, Noelle. Life isn't my fault.

NOELLE: Nothing's your fault, Chris. You just show up, things happen, but nothing ever happens to you. It isn't right.

CHRIS: Take it up with God.

NOELLE: Junk is God.

(NOELLE pulls the plastic bag over CHRIS's head and leaves it on twice as long as the first time. She pulls it off.)

CHRIS: Fix me first. If you're going to kill me, I want to fix.

NOELLE: I'll fix you first. I'll give you a nice shot that'll put you to sleep. Like a sick dog.

CHRIS: Have sex with me. I don't care what you do after that.

NOELLE: How can you still want it? I hate you. I hate every fucking thing about you. You still want to fuck me?

CHRIS: I can't die without doing it.

NOELLE: Well, I'll tell you what. Martin is going to fuck you. That's what you really want.

CHRIS: No.

NOELLE: Oh, yes. Yes it is. Come on, Chris, be honest with your little sister. You've always wanted Martin, haven't you? That's why you're scared of him. That's why you hate him so much. You hate real men. You want to fuck them and they scare you.

CHRIS: I fucked Martin before you ever met him.

NOELLE: He'll kill you when I tell him you said that.

CHRIS: We were partners. I fucked Martin in broad daylight. He didn't need it to be dark.

NOELLE: You don't want to die telling lies. You'll never get to heaven.

CHRIS: Sometimes he cries when he comes. He starts to whisper something and you can never hear it. He whispers, then he comes, then he cries.

NOELLE: I told you that. You heard that from me when I was stoned.

CHRIS: You know I didn't

NOELLE: Martin isn't queer.

CHRIS: Sure. Me neither.

NOELLE: You know what he whispers? My name. He whispers my name.

(She climbs onto the bed and puts the bag over his head after an intense struggle. While CHRIS thrashes about NOELLE takes the money and

stashes it in the garbage container. She returns to the bed and pulls off the bag just before CHRIS blacks out.)

I've got no idea where we are, but we're making damn good time.

(She unlocks the handcuffs, then goes into the bathroom and starts running water in the tub. CHRIS gets up, pulls up his pants, tries to collect himself. NOELLE returns.)

Now the question is, did I call Martin or didn't I? If I was in your shoes, I don't think I'd take any chances. He'll kill you if I want him to. Martin loves me more than he loves you. So pack up and hit the road, brother. We're even. I'm leaving you the clothes on your back. Same as you left me.

CHRIS: You know what you are. You know what you fucking are.

NOELLE: Yeah, I'm tough.

(CHRIS grabs NOELLE and lifts her off her feet. He drops her on the bed and crawls on top of her until his knees are on her shoulders. He has little trouble forcing her hands through the headboard and snapping the cuffs on her wrists. NOELLE struggles, but doesn't speak.)

CHRIS: You fucking brat.

(He picks up the plastic bag used to suffocate him.)

How do you feel, now? Scared?

NOELLE: I fought the law. I fought the law and the law won. Sorry, brother. They say, put a paper bag over his head and fuck him. A *paper* bag. My mistake.

CHRIS: I'm not leaving here without my money.

NOELLE: There's nothing you can do that's going to make

me tell you where it is. You won't find it in a thousand years. I've got a place even the cops can't find.

(CHRIS rips bag.)

I wish you could see how stupid you look. You had it coming. You know you did. You've never even done time, you fucking pussy. Act like a man. You don't want to be bad, you want to be naughty. Wait till I tell Dad you love my boyfriend. You're not going to make me talk and we both know it. Martin could make me, but you can't.

(CHRIS lights a cigarette and picks up teddy bear.)

CHRIS: Martin could make me do lots of things, too.

NOELLE: You have to ruin everything I've ever had. You've always done it, my whole life. You're so jealous.

CHRIS: Maybe.

(CHRIS sits teddy bear on NOELLE's chest.)

I want you to tell little Martin where you hid my money. Martin, she's got my money and she won't give it back. *(He puts the bear's mouth to his ear.)* Martin says you're a bad girl.

NOELLE: You came out here just to tell me about you and him, didn't you? Just so you could wipe out what we have.

CHRIS: You wiped out what I had with him. Think about that. I'm going to do the worst, most horrible thing in the world to you.

NOELLE: I'll fucking die before I tell you where the money is.

(CHRIS blows on the cigarette and puts pillowcase over her head. Parts her legs.)

Go.

> (CHRIS digs in his fingers below her ribs and tickles her beyond what anyone would find comfortable. NOELLE shrieks, twists and turns, begs him to stop. He stops.)

I'll kill you.

> (He digs his fingers into her side again, just enough to give her the message.)

Okay, okay. It's in the fucking garbage. In a fucking milk carton in the fucking garbage.

> (CHRIS takes off pillowcase. MARTIN whispers in CHRIS's ear.)

CHRIS: What? Oh, my goodness.

> (CHRIS gets money from garbage. Phone rings. Long pause. Phone stops ringing.)

I've always been in love with you. Right from forever.

> (CHRIS twists the hundreds in his hand and sticks them into the flame of the candle. He walks into the bathroom with the burning bills and drops them into the toilet. He turns off the bath taps. NOELLE is awestruck and speechless. When CHRIS comes out of the bathroom, she begins to cry.)

Your bath is ready, madam.

NOELLE: It isn't fair. I don't have anything.

CHRIS: Same here.

NOELLE: That was nuts. You're crazy.

CHRIS: I know what crazy is. I paint houses, maybe I'm queer, I marry women who hate me. I'm in love with my sister. I'm not crazy.

> (He undoes handcuffs and NOELLE sits up on the bed. CHRIS sits beside her.)

NOELLE: We can't even fix. The last fix in the world and I can't have it. That was the craziest fucking thing I ever saw in my life.

CHRIS: I'm flattered.

(Takes the necklace from the side table and puts it on the teddy bear.)

NOELLE: Martin, Martin, Martin. I can't stand it.

CHRIS: He never gave me anything this nice. He must really like you.

NOELLE: You're cold. In the middle of your heart, you're ice.

CHRIS: That summer when Doc, Jinks, all those guys were killed, I thought, I *knew* right then, I'd never be as tough as you. You knew every one of them and you were dry-eyed and rock steady. I wanted to get down and bow.

NOELLE: That kid, Larry, when we lived on Mill Street. You stole his silver dollars. They were the only things he had of his father's and his father had just died. You stole them and I thought wow, my brother means business. You and Martin, you were made to be together.

CHRIS: You want to compare sins? We could sit here all night. We were both made for Martin.

NOELLE: We were made for each other.

CHRIS: What are we doing, Noelle?

NOELLE: We're going to take a bath. We have to do something.

CHRIS: It takes more guts to kill yourself than to go on living. It really does.

NOELLE: Maybe. We're not going to kill ourselves with dope, that's for sure.

CHRIS: Tomorrow, if you feel like this, I'll call Dad. I promise.

NOELLE: If I feel like what?

CHRIS: Like you did when you woke up this morning.

NOELLE: You're not as stupid as you look, Chris.

CHRIS: Actually, I am. That's my whole problem. Am I sleeping here?

NOELLE: What kind of girl do you think I am?

(They shed the rest of their clothes, CHRIS gets up and NOELLE hops onto his back. She picks up the one candle that's still burning.)

The only thing, you know what I regret? The fucked-up things I didn't do. That's what makes me feel bad. I feel bad about the bad things I didn't do.

CHRIS: You said it. You said it all.

NOELLE: I've done my best, but I'm not perfect. What can I say? Regrets, I've had a few.

(They disappear into the bathroom.)

(NOELLE returns, dressed as at the top of Act One, facing the audience.)

I heard a joke. This couple, they've got one kid, a boy and he's a perfect little boy. Everything about the kid is great except he won't speak. They take him to doctors, hospitals, they run every test in the world and they don't know what's wrong. One night they're having dinner and the kid pushes his plate away and he says, this is terrible. Well, the parents go nuts. They're crying, hugging him, they're so happy their little boy has finally spoken. His mother, once they've calmed down, his mother says, why now? Why didn't you speak before? The kid says, up to now everything was okay.

When I was about, I was in Grade Five or Six, I used to lie down in the snow in this field behind my school. I had a friend, Linda, one winter we used to go there and lie down in the snow and wait for boys. Linda used to do this, they knew we were there. It was mainly necking, kids' stuff, they'd put their hands under our clothes. There was a guy my brother knew, he liked me, sometimes he'd pull other guys off me and have me all alone. I didn't like him, I liked what he did. You lie down in a field, you're not being choosy. Sometimes it was just me and him, my brother and Linda. The guys, we were lying so close, their shoulders would rub together. I remember that. I don't think about when I was a kid but I remember that.

I haven't been here lately. Yesterday it was, it's been three months. Three months since I fixed, yesterday. This guy Chris, I've known him all my life, he came to visit me. I hadn't seen him in years and years and we were going to score but we changed our minds.

There's things I've done and I just don't feel bad about them. Things I did to people, most of them had it coming. Maybe I'll change my mind about that, maybe I won't. I'm not trying to be normal. Chris is married and that isn't the worst problem we've got, believe me. We got involved after all those years, after our whole lives. Involved.

I've been with guys, a lot of guys, especially after I started using. Before that, I was married. Sometimes we'd fix, me and a guy, and in the dark I'd be kind of nodding in and out and I'd get the idea I was really with Chris. I'd say his name. Chris told me it happened to him as well. So Chris was here except we weren't stoned and the whole night I felt like I had a fever. I'd see his face for a second and this time it really was him and the whole night long I saw the kinds of things you see with a high fever. I woke up in the morning and I felt like I'd crossed the ocean swimming. And in the morning it was still Chris.

We didn't score.

Martin, I don't know where to start. Martin, he's, what can I tell you about Martin? Martin is a stuffed animal.

I have a brother, he's an alcoholic, he drank a long time. I did my first shot, the first time I fixed, it was with a guy he knew. My brother is a drunk, he's a sober drunk now, but it was always junk for him. I've never had a thing for booze. It's sloppy and there's no class to it. But you don't have to rob a bank to get a drink. You don't shoot anyone, stab anyone, you don't go back to the liquor store and break the guy's knees because he ripped you off. You don't get to live like that, drinking. Junk gives you a life. It isn't perfect, maybe, but it gets you out of bed in the morning. It gets me out of bed. I think what fucked my brother up, you've really got to know what it is you want. You can be wired to anything, but you've got to know what does it for you. That's, as far as I'm concerned, that's the whole thing right there.

It's funny, I was thinking about my brother, about when we were kids. I remember when he started drinking, not when he was a kid, he was drunk every night once he started. I said to him, is this what you want? Is it good, as good as the real thing? My brother says, he said, after junk, drinking was like kissing your sister.

He told me, and he drank a lot, he said it never really got him there. It didn't get him where he wanted to go. He drank and drank, he's an alcoholic, but it wasn't the same. It was like, like what he said. I guess you know what he was trying to say. If it's not what you want, if it isn't the real thing, then it's just like kissing your sister.

I guess that pretty well says it all.

The End